Interviewing by Example

Finding the right piece of the puzzle

JANIS P. WHITAKER

Table of Contents

Section 1: Introduction

Section 2: Before the Interview

Section 3: During the Interview

Section 4: After the Interview

Section 5: Legal Issues

Section 6: Appendix

Section 1: Introduction

Purpose

The purpose of this book is to provide you with the tools you will need to prepare for and conduct successful interviews in the workplace. Whether you are a seasoned professional or new to the interviewing realm, this book is for you!

This book will take you step by step through the interview process from preparing for the interview, to asking key questions, to evaluating the candidates, and to making a final decision. The book is interactive and full of information, helpful tools, handy checklists, and great hints.

You will find this useful as a workbook and a learning tool. Make notes in the margins. Write on the pages. Highlight key ideas. It is not a one-time or one-day read. It should be read over time so that you can integrate and practice each step in the process. Use this as a reference book to be applied as circumstances dictate. Draw on it when preparing for your first interview or for your 500th interview. Every time you refer to *Interviewing by Example*, the book will increase in meaning and depth.

I have trained managers and supervisors in interviewing techniques since 1986. I have interviewed my own staff and helped interview for positions in other companies. Without a doubt, this interviewing technique has had a positive influence on thousands of people and numerous companies. It can be used with associations, small offices, nonprofit organizations, and Fortune 500 companies. This technique is straightforward—and it works!

The primary focus of this book is interviewing techniques. It does not discuss how to create applications, recruit, review resumes, check references, provide job offers, or conduct performance evaluations. That will be for another book.

The *Interviewing by Example* technique is based on the premise that past behavior is a good predictor of future behavior. Knowledge of past behaviors and skills does not guarantee future success, but it is a good indicator. Your goal, as an interviewer, is to glean examples of behaviors from your job candidates' past work experiences, education, and life that will demonstrate the particular skills needed for the specific job you are filling. This interview process is designed to easily find out if your candidate is going to fit the needs of your company. *Interviewing by Example* will assist you in your goal of hiring top quality employees, the first time!

You will notice a recurring puzzle theme throughout the pages of this workbook. Let me explain. The interview process is like a big puzzle and you are one of the puzzle "players." There are three different ways to use this puzzle analogy in interviewing. First, your department or company stands as the completed picture (usually found on the top of the puzzle box). The individual pieces of the puzzle are the employees who comprise the department or company picture. When an employee leaves, a portion of the picture is missing. The picture is not complete and it is difficult for the department or the company to run as smoothly as it used to. Your job, as an interviewer or hiring manager, is to find the piece of the puzzle that is missing and be certain that the new employee "fits" into the entire picture. You need to look carefully at the entire picture, see what is missing (what skills and knowledge are missing), and search to find someone who has those attributes to fill the gap. Therefore, during the interview process, you are trying to "find the right piece of the puzzle."

The second way to look at the puzzle analogy is to see the picture on top of the box as the job applicant. Then, your task as an interviewer is to be certain you have a complete picture of the candidate before you make a final decision. You will want to review the resume thoroughly; have multiple people interview the candidate; ask about different skills, knowledge, and level of success; complete a background check; and maybe gather more information before you make a final decision. In other words, you will want to "find all the pieces of the puzzle" before making the final hiring decision.

The third way to use this analogy is to envision eight different steps or pieces needed to complete the *Interviewing by Example* puzzle. These steps are key concepts that must be completed in order to see the complete picture (the applicant, the job skills, the interviewers, and the company). See page 11 for the eight steps to "finding the right piece of the puzzle."

Learning Objectives

After you complete this book, you will be able to:

1. Interview with increased confidence and control
2. Develop customized questions that address the skills needed for the position
3. Make informed decisions about the candidate's responses
4. Hire top quality employees who will meet the needs of your company

By improving the interview process, an organization will not only be able to hire top quality employees, but it will ultimately spend less time interviewing while achieving compliance with legal requirements. The interview process, *Interviewing by Example*, is fair and consistent.

Assessments and Exercises

For maximum effectiveness, complete all the assessments and exercises sprinkled throughout the pages. Assessments are titled **Assess Your Skill** and require you to make decisions and check what seems to be the best choice. The Answer Key in the Appendix provides the correct responses and a brief explanation. Exercises are titled **Time to Write** and these sections require you to write information that will help prepare you for the interview process.

The following symbols identify these portions in the book.

 Assess Your Skill   **Time to Write**

You may write directly in this book or on a pad of paper, use your computer or whatever works best for you. Whichever system you choose, complete each skill assessment and exercise in sequence, since each concept builds upon the one before. You may also choose to copy the exercise pages from the book for your own non-commercial use. If you share this information with others, please credit the author in this way: from *Interviewing by Example*, by Janis P. Whitaker.

Types of Interviews

Behavioral Interviewing

This book addresses behavioral interviewing. An interviewer finds out about the applicant's skills by asking for examples of when the person has used the skill in the past. Examples can be drawn from the workplace, an academic setting, past or current associations, community organizations, or other social or professional settings. The premise of behavioral interviewing is that future success can be predicted based on past successes. This is called *Interviewing by Example*.

Phone Screen

A phone screen can be a useful tool in the interview process. It is a mini-version of a behavioral interview. One major advantage is the time and money saved if a candidate lives far away. By conducting a phone screen, you can determine if the candidate has the basic qualifications to merit bringing the person in for a complete in-house interview. It is a much shorter version of an in-house behavioral interview, and is designed to narrow your focus when it seems there are many qualified candidates. Only those who "pass" the phone screen should be invited to complete the formal in-house interviews.

To prepare for the phone screen, the interview team (see page 9, Who Should Interview) should pick one or two of the **most important** skills necessary for the position. The phone screen can be conducted by a Human Resources professional or another vital member of the interview team. After asking the questions and reviewing the answers, if the candidate does not have sufficient expertise in these areas, then the person is not invited in for full behavioral interviews with the entire team.

Be certain the key skills chosen are absolutely critical to the job. You do not want to screen out a valuable candidate by mistake.

Advantages	Disadvantages
• Short and to the point	• Could ask about the wrong skills
• No meeting room needed	• Poor phone quality
• No scheduling of other interviewers	• Unnatural conversation
• Not influenced by appearance (age, race, dress, etc.)	• Not able to see non-verbal expressions (facial, hand gestures, etc.)
• Pares down large list of candidates	• Difficult to arrange phone time
• Saves money (not flying candidates in for interviews)	• Time zone issues

Phone Screen Checklist

❏ Have resume and job description with you

❏ Introduce yourself
Name, title, company name, position

❏ Explain procedure and length of interview

❏ Review basic job responsibilities

❏ Build rapport; ask general questions

❏ Ask prepared questions

❏ Take notes

❏ Let the person ask questions

❏ Explain the next step in the process and when to expect the next contact

Screening Interview

The screening interview is usually conducted by one person, such as a Human Resources professional who is very aware of the specific job needs. This type of interview is useful when there seem to be many qualified applicants (per the resume screen) for a particular job. Unlike a phone screen, the screening interview is conducted in person. You might look at it as the "first" interview. The screening interviewer completes a full behavioral interview and then determines whether this person should be invited to return for additional behavioral interviews with the designated team members at another time.

Note: Although I do not recommend the following interview methods or types, they are described so you can be aware of other interviews that are used in the workplace.

Panel Interview (group or team interviews)

Panel interviews are prevalent in academic, government, and scientific settings. The basic structure of a panel interview is that several people are interviewing a potential employee at the same time. It may be done around a conference table or not. Essentially, the interviewers are in chairs facing an applicant who sits alone. Many panel interviews have a moderator or facilitator who keeps the process on track and on time. The fundamental concept is that each interviewer asks questions of the applicant and the applicant is expected to answer the questions as they are delivered by each person. Interviewers can ask questions randomly or in sequence (such as interviewer 1, 2, 3, etc.). If your company conducts this type of interview, I recommend that the interviewers use planned, behavioral questions so there is consistency in what is asked of each candidate.

Videotaped Interview

This is a relatively new concept, but it is worth mentioning. It is most often used to avoid travel costs for out-of-town candidates. A candidate is asked questions and is videotaped while answering them, perhaps online. The video is then reviewed by the decision makers, who will compare the video responses of all the candidates to make a decision.

Stress Interview

A stress interview is just what it sounds like—and it is designed to put the job seeker under stress to see how the person reacts. Companies might employ this method if the daily job is truly stressful and they want to observe how the candidate might perform under these circumstances.

Theoretical/Situational Interview

This type of interview asks the job seeker what he or she would do in a particular situation. Scenarios or situations are created to simulate workplace events and the job seeker is judged by the appropriateness of the answers. Though many companies use this method, in my opinion, the answers can be contrived and a person can answer the "right way" through book learning and without actual experience or skills. Just because the person knows the right answer does not necessarily correlate with behavior on the job. In my opinion, this method falls short of the preferred method, *Interviewing by Example*.

Who Should Interview

Interviewing by Example utilizes the "team approach" to interviewing. Ideally, a minimum of three people will interview each applicant. These behavior-based interviews are best conducted by each interviewer independently.

After all interviewers have completed talking to the applicants, the interview team members will meet to discuss their findings in a group meeting (Applicant Review Meeting). Information is shared, discussed, and a group consensus decision is made. It is usually a very robust and powerful process.

When creating an Interview Team, keep the following ideas in mind. All members should be:

- Familiar with the job responsibilities, the skills needed, and the skill level required for the job.
- Trained in *Interviewing by Example* techniques and be willing to use prepared questions.
- Willing to attend the Applicant Review Meeting (ARM).
- Able to portray the company culture and mission statement, explain how the job fits into the company goals, and answer basic questions about the company.
- Knowledgeable about what they legally should and should not ask during an interview.

> *As an HR Generalist, I have been interviewing candidates for 20+ years and often in a very fast-paced environment that required newly hired staff to "hit the floor running." Thus, it was so important to hire the right person. Once I began using these techniques, I became a supporter. I have promoted "behavioral interviewing" with cooperation and acceptance at three companies where I have served as Director/Vice President, Human Resources.*
>
> *—Kathe Houghtaling, VP Human Resources, Biocept, Inc.*

Here are key items all interviewers should know.

All interviewers should:

❏ Know the job

❏ Know the company

❏ Get to know the applicant

❏ Be trained in the *Interviewing by Example* process

In a nutshell, interviewers should be able to determine three basic factors about an applicant. Specifically, you want to find out if the person . . .

1 . . . can do the job

2 . . . will fit into the organization

3 . . . really wants the job

Key Concepts

There are several key concepts/steps involved in the *Interviewing by Example* process, and each step is like "finding the right piece of the puzzle." As previously mentioned, this is the third way to use the puzzle analogy. You can envision the blending together of the eight different steps, or pieces, needed to complete the *Interviewing by Example* puzzle.

These steps are key concepts that must be completed in sequential order to see the complete picture (the applicant, the job skills, the interviewers, and the company). Each step builds into the next step until the best candidate becomes your employee of choice.

See the next page for the eight steps to "finding the right piece of the puzzle."

When all eight steps are completed, the pieces fit together into a puzzle that more clearly reveals the best candidate for the job.

Step	Description
1	**Determine needed skills, knowledge, and behavior**
2	**Recognize past performance**
3	**Create questions that ask about the past**
4	**Complete personal preparation**
5	**Listen for EAR and take notes**
6	**Rate answers independently**
7	**Evaluate with interview team**
8	**Hire top quality employees**

Section 2: Before the Interview

Interviewing Basics

Let's first determine what you know about a few central principles of interviewing. This is not an IQ test, but a few questions to get you thinking about the overall process. You may want to take this assessment again after you have completed this book. There is a blank assessment included in the Appendix, page 67.

 ## Assess Your Skill

Read each statement and then check whether the statement is "True" or "False."

Statement	True ✓	False ✓
1. Don't make a hire/no hire decision based on the resume.		
2. The interviewer should do most of the talking.		
3. Hold all calls and other interruptions during an interview.		
4. The purpose of an interview is to observe how a job seeker reacts under pressure.		
5. Your decision to hire should be based on your first impression.		
6. The best candidates have done the job before at another company.		
7. There should be a time limit on the interview.		
8. You can ask whatever you want in the interview, if you think it is important.		
9. Always have more than one person interview a candidate.		

Answers and explanations can be found in the Answer Key in the Appendix section.

Determine Needed Skills, Experience, and Behaviors

Interviewing by Example takes preparation. The first step of the entire interview process is determining what skills, experience, and behaviors are needed for the person to be successful on the job. This is a crucial part of the entire process; do not skip this step!

 Determine needed skills, experience, and behaviors

Are you sure you do not want to prepare? If you do not determine the correct skills needed to be successful on the job, you will not create the proper questions, which means you will not get the appropriate answers, which will lead to hiring the wrong person!

Therefore, if you determine the correct skills needed to be successful on the job, you will create the proper questions, which means you will get the appropriate answers, which will lead to hiring the right person!

Take heart in this preparation though. As you look ahead to the next time you hire an employee for this position, all the groundwork will be done!

Here is your first assignment. Choose one job that you will use as a model throughout all of the exercises in this book. Become knowledgeable about the position and refer to a job description, if available. As you continue through this book, continue to use this job title. By the end of this book, you will have the practice you need to be a better interviewer, and you will be prepared to interview for this particular job!

> *At Evans Hotels, we look for much more than previous experience or technical expertise. We also hire applicants who smile and who are genuinely friendly during the interview. These are key attributes or skills we desire in our hotel employees. We believe that for certain jobs, it is easier to train someone how to operate our computer systems than to teach them how to be friendly with our guests.*
>
> —Dan Ferbal,
> Corporate Director
> of Human Resources,
> Evans Hotels

Job Title: _____

This part of the preparation should not be completed alone. Gather job experts together to assist you. Who is a job expert? The person who currently performs this job or who formerly did this job, the boss, a coworker, a Human Resources representative, or internal customers—they may all be job experts. Also, have the job description handy (and hope it is up-to-date!).

Together, this group will determine the skills necessary to be successful in this job. This expert group will also determine what "level" of skill or knowledge is needed for the job. This will assist you later in the process, when you are asking your questions. All this will ensure the hiring team is making an informed decision.

Job Title vs. Job Skills

Before you start listing skills, let's look at the difference between a job title and job skills. This may be a challenging concept to understand at first, but let's take it step by step.

What is the difference between a job title and job skills? Think of it as **what** a person does (job title) versus **how** the person performs the job (skills and behaviors needed).

Job title.... is the name of what a person does; the name for the overall work to be accomplished.

Job skills... relate to the specific talents one needs to achieve success in that job. Many different skills are needed to accomplish a particular job.

Here are some samples:

Job Title	Job Skills
Sales Associate	• Building Rapport • Closing a Sale • Overcoming Objections
Administrative Assistant	• Planning and Organizing • Written Communication Skills • Multi-Tasking
Engineer	• Problem Solving • Attention to Detail • Verbal Communication Skills

Assess Your Skill

Let's see if this concept is clear. Determine whether the following words describe a Job Title or Job Skills. Then, check the appropriate box under the column heading.

Words	Job Title ✓	Job Skill ✓
Baker		
Technician		
Organized		
Detail oriented		
Customer Service Representative		
Manager		
Creative		
Truck Driver		
Persistent		

Answers and explanations can be found in the Answer Key in the Appendix section.

Now that you understand and can distinguish between a job title and job skills, let's move forward. With your team of experts, think of at least ten skills that are necessary for a person to be successful in the job you have selected. Take your time and have significant discussions about these skills. Be certain to verify with all the experts that these are the essential skills and abilities. You may want to refer to the Sample Skills list in the Appendix, page 68, for ideas. The list, however, is not comprehensive.

Job Title (from page 15): _____

Time to Write

List ten skills needed to be successful on the job you have chosen.

1. _____

2. _____

3. _____

4. _____

5. _____

6. _____

7. _____

8. _____

9. _____

10. _____

When determining the number of skills needed for a job, the number will vary. Some less demanding jobs may only list 4–5 skills; other positions may need 10–12 or more. The interview team should discuss this point completely and decide the best course of action.

Skill Level

The next step is to discuss and establish the level of expertise needed for each skill. For example, if an applicant must have computer skills, you might ask, "What is meant by that?" This is a crucial question. Use this question often in your discussions.

Here is an example: **Must have computer skills.** As you can see, the two descriptions below use very different levels of expertise and knowledge.

- **Computer skills.** Can add and remove software programs using Windows XP, can create templates in Excel, Word, and PowerPoint, and is able to transfer files using email without supervision.

  or . . .

- **Computer skills.** Can install wireless networking and networking security and can troubleshoot common networking problems without supervision.

Now, you try. Work through each skill (from page 18) individually. Discuss the level of expertise an employee should have in order to be successful in this job. Be certain to set the level as a minimum requirement. In other words, the person would be able to perform the job function working at this specific level. Not, "It would be nice if the person were an expert in everything...!"

 Time to Write

For this exercise, choose five critical skills (page 18) and describe the level of expertise needed to be successful.

Write Job Title (from page 15): _____

Skill	Description of Expertise Needed

Recognize Past Performance

Now that you have listed essential skills and the level of expertise needed, let's look at the next key step to becoming a confident interviewer—recognizing past performance.

 Recognize past performance

Remember, past performance predicts future performance. This statement is vital to the success of this interview process. Let's take a careful look at this statement.

Finding out about and making a hiring decision based on past performance is not a guarantee, but it is a very good predictor of job success. We are creatures of habit. What do you do when you get up in the morning? Do you have a routine? How about when you drive to work? Do you drive the same way each day? Probably so. These habits are helpful to us; it would be annoying if we had to think every morning, "What shall I do first...? Second...?"

Well, when it comes to everyday interactions and work habits, we behave in much the same ways. If you like to make to-do lists and check tasks off as you complete them, that habit will most likely continue wherever you work. If you have a messy desk at your job at ABS Company, when you begin working for XYJ Company, guess what? Your desk will probably be a mess there, too. Indeed, we are creatures of habit.

So, when we are trying to assess the future success of applicants, we are going to take a close look at their past work habits (past skills or past performance). We want to hear examples of how they have worked in the past so we may "predict" how they will work in the future.

Examples:

- If a job applicant could solve complex electrical problems at her last company, then most likely she will bring that skill with her (her performance will be similar to the past).

- Likewise, if she was late to meetings at her last place of employment, then most likely she will be late when working for you.

You cite at least one achievement for each skill. You measure by using numbers, percentages, or dollar amounts for each achievement. You highlight results, not just responsibilities.

—Joyce Lain Kennedy, Resumes for Dummies

What is really meant by past performance? Past performance is something a person has actually done or said. It is not what he wished he had done, could have done, or what he will do in the future. He had to have personally accomplished the task or used a particular skill or had a specific conversation. Again, what did he actually *do* or *say* in the past?

A perceptive interviewer will be able to recognize when a person is talking about the past or the future, or relating a hypothetical situation. So, recognizing the verb tense of the applicant is a vital interviewer skill to develop. It is also important to recognize if the person is telling you about a specific time he did something, as opposed to a generality or vague reference.

Let's assess your ability to recognize past performance. Read each partial statement made by a job applicant. Determine if the person is talking about an actual event in the past (something he actually did or said), or not. Keep in mind, it should also be specific.

 Assess Your Skill

Is this answer describing a specific past performance or task?

	Yes ✓	No ✓
1. "Well, what I usually do in these cases is…"		
2. "I get along with all my co-workers."		
3. "The last project I worked on took me 14 days to complete…"		
4. "Next time I have that problem I am going to…"		
5. "I am a very fast learner."		
6. "Yesterday, my coworker and I finished prioritizing all the shipments by…"		

Answers and explanations can be found in the Answer Key in the Appendix section.

Create Questions That Ask About the Past

Now that you can recognize past performance, let's learn how to recognize and create questions that will guide the applicant to the right direction.

 Create questions that ask about the past

We want to develop questions that will ask the applicant about his past performance (again, not future-oriented or hypothetical questions). For examples of behavioral questions, glance at page 24.

 Assess Your Skill

Do these questions ask about specific past skills/performance?
If not, rewrite the question so it is worded properly.

	Yes ✓	No ✓
1. "How would you organize a shipping warehouse?"		
2. "Give me an example of one of your research projects."		
3. "Have you ever made a presentation to management? Tell me about it."		
4. "Do you meet your deadlines?"		
5. "You have written sales reports before, haven't you?"		
6. "Tell me about a time you worked on a team project."		

Answers and explanations can be found in the Answer Key in the Appendix section.

Time to Write

Now that you can recognize correctly worded questions, let's write a few. Using three skills you named on page 18, create three questions for each skill to determine the job seeker's past performance. Eventually, you will want to create a total of six questions so that each interview team member can ask different questions about the same skill.

Skill:

Question 1:

Question 2:

Question 3:

Skill:

Question 1:

Question 2:

Question 3:

Skill:

Question 1:

Question 2:

Question 3:

Note: Refer to page 24 for Sample Questions. See Appendix, page 69, for template.

Sample Questions

Specific Skill	Question
LISTENING...	Please, give me an example of a time when you had to rely upon verbal instructions to get a job done. If you had problems, how did you overcome them?
INITIATIVE...	Tell me about a project you generated on your own.
DETAIL ORIENTED...	Describe your system for controlling errors in your work.
WRITTEN COMMUNICATION...	What are some of the important reports you have written? Choose one and tell me how you planned and completed it. What feedback did you get?
PLANNING AND ORGANIZING...	How do you keep track of your work and how do you decide your priorities?
CONFLICT RESOLUTION...	Tell me about a time you had to help two people solve a conflict between them. What was the outcome and how did you work with them?
LEADERSHIP...	Can you give me an example of an instance when you had to discipline an employee? Why did you do it and what happened?

Complete Personal Preparation

We have spent a lot of time getting you prepared to ask precise questions when you meet the applicant. However, not only should you have prepared questions for the interviewee, but you should be prepared to answer questions that are commonly asked of interviewers! So, be prepared to not only get information, but also to give information.

4 Complete personal preparation

> *Sometimes we take our interviewing knowledge and skills for granted and depend too much on the spontaneity of the moment. Preparation for each interview can't be stressed enough. We owe a professional interview to those who have put their career in our hands.*
>
> —*Mayor Morris Vance, City of Vista, CA*

The best interviewers have a keen knowledge of the position. They are also knowledgeable about the company and its culture. And, they have a passion and commitment to the company and to finding the best employees. The following checklist will help you prepare to be a great interviewer.

To provide information:

❏ Have available a short explanation of the job to clarify questions from the job seeker, if necessary

❏ Be familiar with specific job skills and how they relate to the position

❏ Review legal boundaries; what you should and should not ask the applicant

❏ Be prepared to answer common questions asked by applicants:

   ❏ Company benefits, salary, payroll contact, etc.
   ❏ Usual hours and expected duties / Flex-time options
   ❏ Supervisor and co-workers
   ❏ Working location and conditions
   ❏ Vacations, sick leave, PTO days
   ❏ Goals of the company and department
   ❏ Opportunities for advancement, training, and development
   ❏ Travel requirements, if any
   ❏ Family support (daycare, etc.)
   ❏ Start date, shift, and/or orientation dates
   ❏ Challenges of the job

Promote Your Company

As noted before, the interview process is a two-way street. While you are gathering relevant information about the potential employee, the applicant is also gathering information about you, your company, and its culture. Applicants will use this information to determine whether your company will be a good place to further their career.

Many of today's candidates are not singularly focused on income, but are concerned about other relevant factors such as a challenging work environment, employee development opportunities, flexible work arrangement for increased work-life balance, fitness and health support, and open communication and recognition in the workplace. The interview process is the ideal time to promote and reinforce the relevant attributes of your business.

Always maintain a professional, yet friendly, atmosphere. How you dress, speak, and act reflects on the company as a whole. To the interviewee, you *are* the company. Know how to respond to the following basic questions. The more you know, the more you will be able to promote your company.

Company Basics

- ❏ Number of employees
- ❏ Year company was established
- ❏ Company locations
- ❏ Products and services
- ❏ Website address
- ❏ Company Mission Statement
- ❏ Parent company, if any
- ❏ Sister companies/subsidiaries
- ❏ Recent awards or honors
- ❏ Recent acquisitions
- ❏ New products or services
- ❏ External customers
- ❏ Competition information
- ❏ Any worthy news

Organize the Interview Team

Though interview team members may want to ask about several skills during the interview, not all interviewers need to ask about every skill. Use the example below to see how the skills could be distributed to different members.

Note that all interviewers will be asking about **Teamwork** and **Developing Others**. This shows that these skills are critical for success on the job.

Also, remember that each interviewer will ask multiple unique questions (minimum of two) about each skill; no two questions should be exactly alike.

> The more interviews we conduct, the more complacent we become. We spend time complaining that candidates are unprepared for interviews. I always wonder how many good candidates we've missed because we're unprepared.
> —Dave Carns, General Manager, Jobing.com

Skills	Interviewer 1	Interviewer 2	Interviewer 3
Teamwork	X	X	X
Developing Others	X	X	X
Initiative	X		X
Attention to Detail	X	X	
Presentation Skills		X	X
One-on-One Communication	X		X

Section 3: During the Interview

The Interview Flow

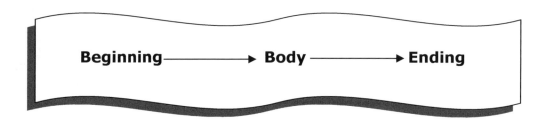

Beginning ──────➤ **Body** ──────➤ **Ending**

Beginning

1. Greet candidate
2. Give overview of process
3. Explain recording

Body

1. Ask general questions
2. Ask specific, planned questions (EAR)
3. Describe organization/ position
4. Invite candidate to ask questions

Ending

1. Inform candidate of next step in process
2. Thank candidate

There are three basic parts to the actual interview. Below is a brief explanation of what should take place in each part: the beginning, the body, and the ending.

Beginning

The beginning of an interview can be quite awkward. Right from the start, you want to set the tone for the rest of the interview. Greet the candidate warmly, shake his or her hand firmly, and introduce yourself clearly. You may want to explain why you are a part of the interview team or what your expertise is. Now is the time to start building your rapport with the applicant. See some rapport-building ideas on page 33.

Next, provide the applicant with a quick overview of what is about to transpire. You may also want to explain how long the interview will be. However, I don't always do this, just in case I want to cut the interview short.

Here is a sample script: "First, I will ask you a few general questions about your work and education (if appropriate), then I will ask you more specific planned questions about your past work experiences. When I have finished, if you wish, I will tell you about our organization and the specific job. Then, I will provide time for you to ask me questions. During the interview, I will be taking notes so I can recall your answers to the questions. Are you ready to begin?"

Body

Now is the time to ask a few general questions to set the person at ease. Ask the candidate simple questions that are easy to answer such as, "Can you please tell me about some of the main responsibilities at your last job?" or "What did you like best about working at your last job?" These questions will be straightforward and you will get fairly short and simple answers.

As you see the applicant beginning to feel more at ease, and you notice how he or she answers your questions, it is time to proceed to your planned, behavioral questions. Explain that you are about to change modes and ask very specific questions about his or her past work history. Sometimes it is helpful to explain EAR (described on page 36). The "body" section is where you will spend most of your interview time, and you will want to take copious notes so you can recall the conversation later.

> ...*relative to behavioral interviewing and the heart of what it is all about... here is a very important lesson I have learned: You get what you asked for!*
>
> – *Patrick W. Lavey, Employee Relations Manager, Abbott Vascular*

After obtaining all the information you need, if it is desired, you may explain more about the position and provide insights into the company. Remember, you are selling the company as well as interviewing the candidate.

The last part of this section of an interview is when you take the opportunity to invite the applicant to ask you questions. Although some interviewers hold it against candidates if they don't have questions, do not judge candidates too harshly for few or no questions. (The exception would be a high level position where these candidates should have done their homework and are expected to have some insightful questions!).

Ending

Ending an interview can be a bit awkward also. A nice segue for finishing the interview is to inform the candidate of the next steps in the process. Some examples of next steps are going to the next interviewer, returning to the front lobby, and completing additional forms or supplementary paperwork.

Finally, thank the candidate for taking the time to interview with the company and shake hands. Remember to maintain a friendly and professional attitude at all times.

Establish Rapport

Many job seekers arrive at an interview with some fear and anxiety. As you know, it is difficult to think clearly when your mind is racing a million miles an hour! So, your job as an interviewer is to create a relaxed, open, and positive atmosphere for the candidate. *Interviewing by Example* is most effective when the interviewer has a positive rapport with the job seeker.

Maintain a Positive Atmosphere

In the beginning of the interview, ask general questions to set the applicant at ease. The first couple of minutes should be spent asking questions that are easy to answer. This allows time for you to get the applicant talking freely and comfortably without having to think very much. For example:

"Did you have trouble finding our building?"
"Would you like water or coffee?"
"Tell me about your major responsibilities at your last job."
"What did you like about your last job?"

If the applicant is a recent student, ask about favorite classes, teachers, etc. Maintain a conversational style throughout the interview. When using *Interviewing by Example*, you will need to gain a lot of detail about what a candidate has accomplished in the past. The more comfortable the candidate is, the easier it will be to get important details. Obtaining pertinent information should be similar to having a casual conversation with someone, except you have a definite goal in mind.

The following comments can be effectively used for maintaining a positive, comfortable atmosphere. These comments can be used to make transitions between questions, used when you first meet the person, or used when the person is having trouble sharing an example.

- "May I get you some water or coffee?"
- "Do you need a quick break?"
- "That sounds great."
- "That's interesting. Tell me more."
- "We all have trouble sometimes...."
- "That was a tough question, let's try...."
- "Sometimes these questions can be difficult...."
- "I know it is hard when...."
- "I bet that made you feel good...."
- "I see at your last job, you were a....
- "Could you tell me a bit more?"
- "Don't worry about that...."
- "Thank you, that was helpful."
- "Good luck on the rest of your interviews."

Control Time

Your time together should feel like a casual conversation. It is important that you control the time and content of the interview. You need to establish rapport and maintain a positive atmosphere. You must be sensitive to time constraints at all times.

Determine the time limit for an interview and stick to it as closely as possible. Depending on the type of interview, the length can vary from 10 minutes to 75 minutes or more. The interview time is determined by the type of interview, the level of the job, the number of skills being asked to share, and the total number of interviewers. Interview times vary greatly and the interview team should discuss what is best for each situation.

There is no ideal time frame, but here are general recommendations:

Phone screen interview	—	10 to 15 minutes
Screening interview	—	20 to 30 minutes
Individual behavioral interview	—	30 to 50 minutes

Timing Challenges

There are two main "applicant challenges" to address when keeping track of your time. First, there is the applicant who rambles on and on, and second, there is the applicant who is very quiet or shy. With either of these interviewees, you may not get enough information about the person's work skills and experience to make a proper decision. There are hints for collecting information from each style of job seeker on the next page.

The Rambler

- Set the stage for the entire interview by explaining you have a limited amount of time to complete the interview.
- Politely interrupt the person by asking the next question or telling the person you have enough information.
- Explain that shorter answers are okay and if you want more information, you will ask additional questions.
- Lay out the entire E-A-R concept, so the person can tailor answers to that format.

The Observer

- Use open-ended questions, comments, and phrases to draw out more information. "What then?" "Really?" "Yes, what happened next?"
- Again, set the stage for the interview by explaining what you are looking for, such as, "Tell me about a time when...."
- Be silent and listen. Many times, because you are silent the other person will start to speak. Few people enjoy sitting in silence, especially in an interview.

Listen for EAR and Take Notes

You are in the interview, you know the job title and skills needed, and you have specific job-related questions to ask. But, what do you do after you ask the questions?

 Listen for EAR and take notes

Listening is an essential skill when interviewing. You must listen to the answer to be certain the candidate understood your question correctly. You also need to listen for an example of past performance and make certain all parts of the question are answered. All of this, plus you need to take notes, keep eye contact, and maintain a friendly rapport with the applicant! Whew!

After asking a question, you will be listening for three things: Example, Action, and Result. Example means what was "going on" or what was the situation or task the person had to complete. This is the starting point. After finding out what the Example is, then you want to find out what the person did or said (Activity or Action) regarding that situation. Lastly, and most importantly, find out the Result of the action. In other words, find out what happened as a result of what the person did or said.

Here is a quick summary:

E... Example (what was going on or what was the situation)

A... Action or activity (what did he do or say)

R... Result (what happened as a result of what he did or said)

Follow-Up Questions

Follow-up questions are any questions asked after the planned question. These questions help guide the interviewee in answering all parts of the EAR. All questions should be open-ended, which means the question cannot be answered by either "Yes" or "No" (or with one word). An explanation usually follows an open-ended question.

Don't ask questions that the candidates will answer with a simple "Yes" or "No," but rather ask open-ended questions, getting them to tell you a story. This gives more insight into their abilities.

—Brook Murphy,
Staffing Specialist

Examples:

Closed question: "Is blue your favorite color?"

Open-ended question: "Explain what color is your favorite and why."

Examples of open-ended, follow-up questions:

- "Can you tell me a specific time when that happened?"
- "What did you do?"
- "Tell me more about...."
- "How did it end?"
- "Please give me an example."
- "What was your role in....?"
- "What did you say?"
- "How did you handle that?"
- "What happened next?"
- "Why did you do that?"
- "What happened as a result?"
- "How did that affect....?"
- "Please explain...."
- "Help me understand...."

Let's assess your ability to recognize this part of the interviewing process.

 Assess Your Skill

Read each statement to determine what information you have.
Is it E, A, or R? Or, a combination of E-A-R? Circle all that apply.

 E A R │ 1. "It was my job to watch the computer readout on the machine."

E A R │ 2. "The entire department was submitting different paperwork for the same process. They asked me to design a template for the department. I did and now all the people in the company use it."

E A R │ 3. "I completed the paperwork for my boss."

E A R │ 4. "If it were to happen again, I would discuss the matter in private. That would have made a big difference."

E A R │ 5. "The customer requested another product, so I sent it to them with a new quote. I had to adjust the final paperwork, but I still made the deadline."

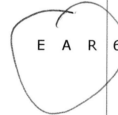 E A R │ 6. "I was getting tired of the clerks coming to me asking what they should do next after they finished a job. So, I set up a plan that I called 'Daily Duties.' Under the plan, each clerk got a list of five ongoing projects that he or she could work on when there was a lull in the work. After using the plan for one month, our output increased and the clerks did not come to me as often."

 E A R │ 7. "I am highly motivated, get along with people, and really care about the quality of my work. I've done lots of things to increase the quality in the department. I just couldn't be happy with a job that didn't challenge me."

Answers and explanations can be found in the Answer Key in the Appendix section.

Taking Notes

As you ask questions and listen to the answers, it is vital that you write the information down. It is virtually impossible to recall all the details for each candidate without taking useful notes.

Though some people are natural "note takers," many people are not. *Interviewing by Example* relies upon recalling many details. Do not write every detail or every word. However, write enough detail that you will be able to look at your notes the next day and be able to recall the specifics of the conversation. Take a few moments after the interview to fill in gaps in your notes so they will be more valuable later.

If note taking is a skill you need to work on, practice taking notes while you are talking on the phone or while you are watching TV. This will give you the practice you will need to take interview notes while, at the same time, keep eye contact with job applicants.

- Try to capture and record the significant details of the conversation or event.
- Look at your notes page only when necessary.

Write on a separate piece of paper, never on the resume or the application. Be certain to keep your notes private so the applicant cannot see your written comments. Let the person focus on his or her answers and not on what you are writing down. All comments in your notes should be job-related.

For example, do not write "She has children" or "He uses a wheelchair." That could come back to haunt you should any discrimination charges arise later on. Even doodles may be interpreted as discriminatory if examined later! For more information on this subject, refer to references in the Appendix, pages 70–71.

Try this simple format for recording your notes.

Skill:

Q1:

E	A	R

Q2:

E	A	R

Q3:

E	A	R

Q4:

E	A	R

Q5:

E	A	R

Interview Close

Closing the interview is as important as the first impression you created when you initially met the candidate. Maybe it is even more important. End with a positive remark for the candidate, but be careful not to make any promises about employment.

Explain the next step in the day's process, or, if you are the last interviewer, tell the candidate when to expect to hear about a decision.

No matter how the interview progressed, say good-bye with a firm handshake, smile warmly, and thank the candidate for coming in. Whether you hire this person or not, leave the candidate with a positive impression of you and your company.

I think it is always important for the people doing the interview to never lose sight that they could be in that interview seat and to treat candidates with respect and care. Everyone should leave an interview feeling good—never put down or belittled. The people might not have the experience or skills you are currently looking for, but they should be able to speak well of the experience, so they talk positively about you and your company to their friends.

—Lori Schmitt,
President, Integrity Staffing, Inc.,
Specializing in Human Resources

Interview Day Reminders

The day has finally arrived and it is almost time to meet the potential employee face-to-face. Use the following handy checklist to help you with your interview preparation.

Interview Day Preparation Checklist

Do you have . . .

- ❏ Job description
- ❏ Knowledge of skills needed for the job and what level is required by applicant
- ❏ Resume
- ❏ Application
- ❏ Prepared questions
- ❏ Paper and pen for recording answers (EAR)
- ❏ Quiet room reserved
- ❏ Literature about your company/department (if appropriate)

Do you know . . .

- ❏ The candidate's interview schedule (your time confirmed)
- ❏ Salary and benefits information (if appropriate)
- ❏ Who the other interviewers are
- ❏ When and where other interviews are being held
- ❏ What the next step in the process is for the candidate
- ❏ When/where the Applicant Review Meeting is scheduled

Interviewing Dos and Don'ts

Do	Don't
• Have a quiet place to interview	• Rely upon your memory
• Be prepared	• Ask multiple-part questions
• Ask open-ended questions	• "Feed" answers to candidates
• Ask for specific examples of skills	• Talk too much
• Be patient	• Make decisions too quickly
• Listen for EAR answers	• Discuss non-work related issues
• Take notes	• Be afraid to ask follow-up questions
• Control interview length	• Ask "Yes" or "No" questions
• Provide positive information about company	• Joke about coworkers, boss, things that happen at the company, etc.
• Maintain positive atmosphere	• Allow applicant to see your notes
• Prepare for applicant review meeting	• Write on the resume or application

Section 4: After the Interview

Rate Answers Independently

One of the last tasks to master when *Interviewing by Example* is the rating process. The table on page 47 shows the rating scale. After completing the interview, you will need to go over your notes and rate the candidate's skills using the rating table.

 Rate answers independently

This initial rating is completed independently and based on your planned questions and notes. For example, look at all the questions you asked about "leadership." Keep in mind the skill level you are looking for and rate the applicant on that skill. Let's imagine the answers you transcribed meet your minimum desired skill requirement. The overall rating would be a "4." See example below.

Proceed with each skill. Read your notes, recall the complete answers, and rate the skill in its entirety using the 1–6 rating system. These rating numbers, along with your notes, will be the basis for your discussion regarding the interview in the Applicant Review Meeting. Be certain to rate all the skills and be prepared to explain to others how you determined the rating.

Skill: *Leadership*		*4*
Q1: *Specific question about leadership...?*		
E Comments.......................	**A** Comments.......................	**R** Comments........................ ....
Q2: *Another specific question about leadership...?*		
E Comments.......................	**A** Comments.......................	**R** Comments........................ ....

All interviewers should complete this process for each applicant they interview. Their ratings should reflect the skill expertise decided upon in the initial planning meeting.

Do NOT rate candidates against each other at this point. That process will take place when making the final decision.

Applicant Rating System

Rating	Description
6	**Exceptional Skills**—extremely skilled, may be overqualified if too many skills are ranked here
5	**Exceeds Standard**—above average skills and experience
4	**Meets Standards**—can perform in this area, meets our standard
3	**Slightly Below Standard**—does not meet minimum skill level, however may be able to compensate with coaching, mentoring, or training
2	**Definitely Below Standard**—unacceptable, needs too much training
1	**Unacceptable**—not be to considered, no skills evident
N	**No information**—unable to obtain information

Evaluate With Interview Team

After each interviewer has completed his/her rating process, it is time to convene for the Applicant Review Meeting (ARM). All interviewers should bring their individual ratings and their notes taken during the interview.

 Evaluate with interview team

It is best to have the Applicant Review Meeting in a location with no interruptions and where the ratings can be posted in a central location for all to see (e.g., whiteboard, flip chart, computer projection). The discussion flow will be easier if all scores are visible.

It is important that the interview team members understand their role. They are the actual decision makers for a hire/no hire decision. Open, frank information sharing is essential in the ARM. These discussions will be the basis for hiring your top quality employee.

Post everyone's ratings so they can be seen by all (see example on page 50). After the posting, discussions can begin. Each interviewer gives a brief explanation of why he or she rated the applicant with that particular number on each skill. The explanation should be short and to the point, yet with enough detail to reveal the reasoning behind the score.

Discuss one skill at a time. After all interviewers have explained their score for one skill, discuss what the consensus rating will be. Remember, consensus means that everyone agrees with the "new" rating. The consensus score is NOT an average of the individual ratings! There is no math involved in this process. When the group agrees with the final rating on one skill, they should proceed to the next skill.

The discussions carry on this way until all the chosen skills are discussed and everyone agrees to the consensus rating, as illustrated in the same example on page 50.

When all the ratings for one candidate are complete, the discussion progresses to the next candidate. Follow these same steps as outlined above for each person interviewed for the job.

Follow these helpful guidelines when you meet as a group to discuss the candidate at the ARM.

Applicant Review Meeting

❑ All interviewers should bring the notes taken during the interview and their individual rating scores.

❑ Have the job description handy.

❑ Discuss the most important skills first; if a candidate's rating is low, no additional discussion needs to occur.

❑ Let all interviewers share and explain their ratings.

❑ Be open-minded during discussions.

❑ Discuss each skill independently. Complete one skill and then advance to the next.

❑ The final score on a skill should be a consensus score; there is NO averaging!

❑ Consensus means that everyone agrees with the score.

❑ Do not change individual ratings; the consensus score will reflect any rating change.

❑ Experiences that are recent and more job-related carry more significance.

❑ If two candidates have equal strengths, decide who will have the final hiring decision after all discussions have ended. (The final decision maker is usually the hiring manager.)

❑ Interviewers should save notes and ratings for possible follow-up discussions and for legal reasons. See your Human Resources department for further clarification.

Applicant: Leigh Gertsen

Job Skills	JPW	DMF	MLE	Consensus
Planning and Organizing	2	2	3	2
Communication	4	4	4	4
Leadership	5	3	4	5
Initiative	N	5	4	4
Analysis	4	4	5	6

The completed chart above represents what might be a final product after the Applicant Review Meeting. It illustrates how to capture the individual ratings and final consensus scores of the three interviewers of the candidate, Leigh Gertsen. On the left, the skills are listed and on the top are the initials of those who conducted the interviews. Under each interviewer's name are the individual ratings decided upon before coming to the meeting. The consensus rating, which is derived from the interviewer discussions, is listed to the far right.

Step-by-step procedure in review:
- Each interviewer rates the applicants individually on the Job Skills and brings those scores to the ARM.
- All ratings are posted, so everyone at the ARM can see the data.
- Each skill is discussed one-by-one. The interviewers explain why they rated the skill by sharing the questions they asked and the answers obtained.
- After all interviewers explain their rating for a skill, the first discussion begins.
- Interviewers should keep in mind the level of expertise required for each skill.
- After discussing a skill, the consensus score should be agreed upon by all interviewers and posted. Do not alter the individual ratings; the consensus score reflects the combined viewpoint.
- Once one skill is complete, proceed to the next skill until they are all discussed and the consensus scores are recorded.

- After all skills are rated, the next discussion begins.
- Discuss whether this candidate meets the qualifications for this position and then whether the candidate should continue in the process.
- Proceed through each applicant in the same manner.
- After all applicants have been discussed, it is time to make a final decision. See the Decision Time section below for that process.

An exception to this procedure is illustrated in the Leigh Gertsen chart on page 50. Let's say the interview team decided the most important skills needed for the job are Planning and Organizing. There would be no need to discuss the remaining four skills after reviewing the ratings for Planning and Organizing. Why? Because the consensus rating for Planning and Organizing—rating of "2"—tells us that this person does not have the minimum skills necessary to perform this job function. No other discussion would be needed.

Also note in the same example, the consensus score can move up or down according to the quality of the discussion in the Applicant Review Meeting. The final score accurately reveals the strengths of the applicant if the interviewers have gathered enough information and are able to share their information openly. Agreeing to a consensus score can be difficult at times. Don't let the exact numbers cloud the process; do the best you can and remain open to everyone's ideas and comments.

Decision Time

Final step! It is **now** time to compare applicant to applicant. The people who were involved in the interview process should thoroughly confer and understand what is needed for an employee to be successful on the job. View the ratings, evaluate the strengths and weaknesses, evaluate the salary demands, and make a decision based on the findings of the entire team.

Remember, do not add consensus numbers/ratings together or complete any mathematical calculations! The numbers act as a point of discussion only. The numbers reflect the level of competence for a particular skill per the requirements of the job. Judge each skill independently as it relates to the job.

If, after the discussions, more than one candidate appears qualified, it is a common practice to allow the hiring manager to make the final decision. However, the hiring team should settle on who has the final decision or how the final choice is made.

Hire Top Quality Employees

Notify Your Top Candidates

Act quickly. Call your top candidate as soon as a decision is made. You could lose a top quality employee to the competition if you are slow to act on your choice.

 Hire top quality employees

When contacting your top candidate, be aware that this could become a negotiating process. Many of the top job seekers today know they have a choice of where to work. They will want to discuss several topics before making a commitment. Topics such as salary, benefits, working conditions, location, independence, family support, and development opportunities are common. Don't be afraid to sell the position and your company, but be keenly aware of what you can and cannot promise. Contact your legal department or Human Resources professional for further guidance about negotiating with applicants.

Offer Letters

When a top candidate has been notified by phone, follow up with a letter confirming the start date and the compensation mutually agreed upon. State the compensation in monthly or weekly terms. The courts have determined if you state an annual wage, then you may be obliged to keep the employee for one year!

Follow legal guidelines when creating an offer letter. Offer letters may create a binding contract between your company and the employee because of the way the offer is worded. My main recommendation is this: Be certain an experienced employment law attorney reviews and approves your company's offer letters to avoid any miscommunication or misrepresentation between you (the employer) and the candidate (the employee).

Inform Other Candidates

Once your preferred candidate has accepted the position, be courteous and let those not chosen know their status as well. Remember that these candidates could be interviewing for a number of positions, and might be waiting to hear from you before making other decisions. Calls are not necessary here, a card or letter will do.

Be sure to inform the candidates about:
- The company name
- Position the candidate interviewed for
- Whether the company keeps applications on file (and if they do, for how long)

Thank candidates for their time and simply explain that either their qualifications did not meet your criteria at this point or that the position is filled. Though all applicants should be notified, you are not obligated to explain the specific reasons for not hiring them. In fact, you may want to stay away from detailed information to avoid possible future legal issues. Do wish candidates success in their continued job search.

Continuous Improvement

The following self-evaluation form can help you identify your strengths and areas for improvement after each interviewing experience. Be certain to read through the assessment each time you conduct an interview to confirm that you are still a peak performer.

 Assess Your Skill

Rate yourself. Check the appropriate column regarding your interviewing skills. Excellent (+), OK, or Needs Improvement (−).

	+	OK	−
1. Prepared behavioral questions based on job skills in advance			
2. Arrived on time to interview			
3. Established rapport by asking easy questions at first			
4. Outlined interview process to candidate			
5. Took notes and maintained eye contact			
6. Maintained control of content and time			
7. Let the candidate do most of the talking			
8. Listened carefully to obtain EAR			
9. Asked open-ended, follow-up questions			
10. Avoided legal issues			
11. Answered applicant's questions thoroughly			
12. Closed interview on a positive note and explained next steps			
13. Used notes to rate applicant answers			
14. Brought notes to ARM			
15. Listened to other interviewers in ARM			

If you answered excellent (+) to all the questions, congratulations! Keep up the good work! Otherwise, it looks like you have room for some degree of improvement!

Assess Your Skill

Rate your company by checking the "Yes" or "No" column.

	Yes ✓	No ✓
1. Is the interview process smooth and professional?		
2. Are applicants contacted in a timely manner for interviews?		
3. Are all interviewers trained in the *Interviewing by Example* process?		
4. Do they utilize multiple interviewers?		
5. Do interviewers come prepared to the interviews?		
6. Is the location for interviews professional and private?		
7. Do all interviewers have valuable, positive information to offer the applicant about the company, its culture, and opportunities?		
8. Are interviewers aware of the legal aspects of interviewing?		
9. Are interviewers prepared with their notes and ratings in ARM?		
10. Is there a timely follow-up process?		

If you answered "No" to any of these questions, you may want to consider sharing the concepts of this book with the decision makers at your company or contact J P Whitaker & Associates for an in-house *Interviewing by Example* workshop.

Section 5: Legal Issues

Background

There are many state and federal labor laws designed to protect workers from hiring discrimination. There are hundreds of federal laws that address applicant rights and selection. It would be impossible to address all of these in this book, therefore only a few significant laws will be noted. Please check with a qualified attorney or the legal department at your company to be certain you are complying with the employment laws in your state, as laws do vary state-by-state.

Discrimination is the basis for all these laws. The laws are enacted so that an employer cannot discriminate against anyone who is considered to belong to a "protected class." Though it is not unlawful to ask most questions, you must still be extremely careful what you ask and why.

When it comes to discrimination, it is what the employer might *do* with the answer that comes into question. My rule of thumb is, "When in doubt, don't ask."

The best advice about asking questions in an interview is to only ask BFOQs— Bona Fide Occupational Questions. In other words, your question must ask about legitimate job requirements, or they must be considered a "business necessity." However, this should not be a problem for you if you stay true to *Interviewing by Example* because all the questions you ask will be about specific job skills.

Here is a brief review of a few major laws impacting employment. See Appendix, pages 70–72, for further resources and information.

Civil Rights Act of 1964

The Civil Rights Act of 1964, enacted by Congress, has set the groundwork for most anti-discrimination laws. Specifically, Title VII of that Act refers to labor and employment. Numerous other Acts have been implemented since 1964 that address discrimination issues such as race, sex, age, religion, disability, national origin, etc.

EEOC

In 1978, the EEOC (Equal Employment Opportunity Commission) was tasked with ending employment discrimination. The EEOC developed the Uniform Guidelines for Selection Procedures to help interviewers interpret Federal statutes.

ADA

The American Disabilities Act (ADA) of 1990 is similar to Title VII of The Civil Rights Act. ADA specifically addresses disabled persons and provides guidelines about making reasonable accommodations in the workplace.

Assess Your Skill

Check "thumbs up" (yes) or "thumbs down" (no) about whether you can ask each of the following questions during the interview.

Question	👍	👎
1. How old are you?		
2. Do you wish to be addressed as Miss, Mrs., or Ms?		
3. Many of our employees are Catholic. Do you think you'd have a problem with that?		
4. How many children do you have? If they are young, do they go to daycare?		
5. That's an unusual name. What country is that from?		
6. Many days we have to work overtime. Will that be a problem?		
7. What schools have you attended and when?		
8. Your job requires you to lift 40-pound boxes. Do you have any condition that would prevent you from performing this function?		

Answers and explanations can be found in the Answer Key in the Appendix section.

Checklist for Interviewers

Are you and the other interviewers at your company aware of the following issues that can affect questions asked in an interview? Listed below are some key subject areas you may want to avoid. This list is not complete.

Remember, **when in doubt, don't ask.**

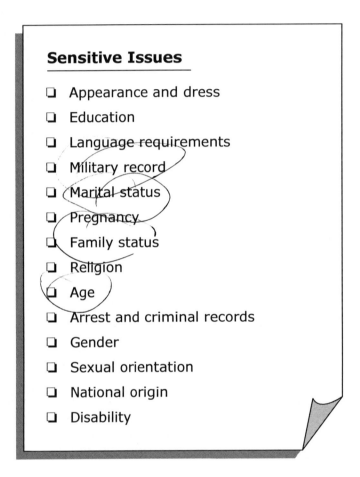

Sensitive Issues

- ❏ Appearance and dress
- ❏ Education
- ❏ Language requirements
- ❏ Military record
- ❏ Marital status
- ❏ Pregnancy
- ❏ Family status
- ❏ Religion
- ❏ Age
- ❏ Arrest and criminal records
- ❏ Gender
- ❏ Sexual orientation
- ❏ National origin
- ❏ Disability

Interviewing Applicants With Disabilities

Since the enactment of the Americans with Disabilities Act of 1990, employers must be aware of how to treat applicants with disabilities during the interview process. You can ask people about their *abilities,* but you can't ask about their *disabilities*. This means that you can ask how an applicant plans to perform each function of the job, but you cannot ask whether the applicant has any disabilities that will prevent him or her from performing each function.

When an employee has a disability, the employer must explore all possibilities of reasonable accommodation prior to rejecting the person for a job or making any employment-related decision. An accommodation is reasonable if it does not impose an undue hardship on the employer's business. The Job Accommodation Network specifically addresses how to meet the needs of disabled employees. (See Appendix, page 71, for their services.)

Here are a few more practical tips when interviewing persons with a disability:

- Shake hands and make direct eye contact as you would with any other applicant.
  - Do not squeeze someone's hand too hard if the person has arthritis or other painful hand problems.
  - If appropriate, shake hands left-handed (missing limb, paralysis, etc.).

- If the applicant is sitting in a wheelchair, do not push or touch the wheelchair unless you ask permission first or the person asks you to assist in some way.
  - Move furniture or obstacles that may impede movement.

- Most important! Keep the interview centered on the applicant's skills and abilities related to the job, not on the disability or what the person cannot do.
  - Ask prepared behavioral questions and it will alleviate this issue.

- If an applicant is deaf and has an interpreter, speak directly to the applicant and not to the interpreter.
  - If there is no interpreter, face the applicant at all times. If the person looks away, tap the person to get his or her full attention.
  - Do not shout, but speak clearly.
  - If some communication is unclear, write notes.

- When interviewing someone who is blind, identify yourself and any others who may be present.
  - When shaking hands, indicate you are ready by saying, "May I shake your hand?" and then wait for a response. Take his or her hand when it is extended.
  - When walking to an interview location, offer your arm and let the person place his or her hand or arm on top of your arm. As you are walking, identify upcoming turns, doors, steps, etc. in advance. Describe where the person is to sit by saying, "The chair is two steps directly in front of you."

- If the applicant has a physical disability that hampers walking, (e.g., cane, limp, etc.), keep pace with the person and do not speed ahead.

This information is not comprehensive nor is it offering any legal advice. Please contact your company's legal department or your Human Resources department for further explanation and legal guidance.

Section 6: Appendix

Answer Key

Assess Your Skill (Page 14)

1. **True**—Resumes can be deceiving; many are created by professional resume writers. Use the resume as a tool to ask more in-depth question about a person's past. Your job is to find out how the person performs his or her job, not just what the person did on the job.

2. **True**—The purpose of an interview is to gather as much information from the candidate as possible in a short amount of time. Use your time wisely and let the candidate tell you about his or her experiences and skills.

3. **True**—*Interviewing by Example* is a focused process built on trust and rapport. Do not let outside influences interrupt your conversation and interview flow. Also, you will present a more professional atmosphere by not being interrupted.

4. **False**—The purpose of an interview is to gain information about the applicant's past work experience. Most applicants are already nervous; your job is to make applicants feel comfortable so they will converse freely with you.

5. **False**—Unfortunately, our first impressions are not always the right impressions. Be certain to gather information from all sources (resume, other interviewers, your interview, references, etc.) before making a final decision.

6. **False**—Just because they had a certain job at another company does not mean they were proficient or successful. Do not eliminate (or hire) an applicant solely on prior job titles; look closely at the skills used and prior experience. Think about your own experiences with co-workers. Are they all excellent workers?

7. **True**—The best interviews have time limits. They are also very focused in gathering information about a candidate. Plan your time and the time of the job seeker wisely.

8. **False**—Refer to Section 5: Legal Issues.

9. **True**—Having more than one interviewer gathering information about a candidate allows a better chance of gaining all the details you need to make a good decision.

Assess Your Skill (Page 17)

Words	Job Title ✓	Job Skill ✓
Baker	✓	
Technician	✓	
Organized		✓
Detail oriented		✓
Customer Service Representative	✓	
Manager	✓	
Creative		✓
Truck Driver	✓	
Persistent		✓

Assess Your Skill (Page 21)

1. No—The word "usually" is not specific enough. Ask the person about a specific time when he or she did something.
2. No—This is a general statement where you need to ask about a specific example of a time the person "got along with coworkers."
3. Yes—The person is talking about a specific project in the past.
4. No—This is a future-oriented statement, not past experience.
5. No—This statement can be used to ask a behavior question though. For instance, "Can you give me an example of a time when you had to learn something quickly?"
6. Yes—The person is about to tell you a story about something he or she actually did.

Assess Your Skill (Page 22)

1. No—The word "would" refers to the future and is not an example of past experience. You might ask how the person has organized a shipping warehouse before.
2. Yes—This question is asking about a specific job skill that was used in the past.
3. Yes—Excellent question asking about a specific skill.
4. No—This question is a closed-ended question (answerable with one word). It also cues the applicant to the answer. Of course, the person will say, "Yes." A better question might be, "Please tell me about the last difficult deadline you had to meet and how did you do it."
5. No—This is a closed-ended question and it also "feeds" the desired answer, "Yes."
6. Yes—This question asks about the past, it is specific, and it asks about what the candidate actually did or said.

Assess Your Skill (Page 38)

1. **E**—This sounds like the beginning of a story or example. Need to ask follow-up questions to determine the rest of the example.

2. **E-A-R**—Complete answer.

    E—"The entire department was submitting different paperwork for the same process.

    A—They asked me to design a template for the department.

    R—I did, and now all the people in the company use it."

3. **A**—Not only do you not have all of the answer, but you might want to ask what "paperwork" the person completed.

4. **Nothing**—This answer is explaining what the person would do in the future. Though this might be an indicator of hindsight, it is not an acceptable example of past behavior.

5. **E-A-R**—Complete answer.

    E—"The customer requested another product,

    A—so I sent it to them with a new quote. I had to adjust the final paperwork,

    R—but I still made the deadline."

6. **E-A-R**—Complete answer.

    E—"I was getting tired of the clerks coming to me asking what they should do next after they finished a job.

    A—So, I set up a plan that I called 'Daily Duties.' Under the plan, each clerk got a list of five ongoing projects that he/she could work on when there was a lull in the work.

    R—After using the plan for one month, our output increased and the clerks did not come to me as often."

7. **Nothing**—This answer lists skills, but it doesn't give a specific example of how the person used his or her skills. Follow up with a specific question to get an example.

Assess Your Skill (Page 59)

The answers below list the discrimination law or protected class that it refers to.

1. **No**—Age
2. **No**—Marital Status
3. **No**—Religion
4. **No**—Family Status
5. **No**—National Origin
6. **Yes**—BFOQ
7. **No**—Age (cannot ask "when")
8. **No**—Disability (cannot use the phrase "any condition")

Remember, there may be exceptions. If a question is a "Bona Fide Occupational Question" (BFOQ), an interviewer can ask it. Consult your legal department for further explanations.

Interviewing Basics / Assessment Template

Blank Assessment. May be used after completing this entire book to assess your knowledge of central principles of interviewing.

 Assess Your Skill

Read each statement and then check whether the statement is "True" or "False."

Statement	True ✓	False ✓
1. Don't make a hire/no hire decision based on the resume.		
2. The interviewer should do most of the talking.		
3. Hold all calls and other interruptions during an interview.		
4. The purpose of an interview is to observe how a job seeker reacts under pressure.		
5. Your decision to hire should be based on your first impression.		
6. The best candidates have done the job before at another company.		
7. There should be a time limit on the interview.		
8. You can ask whatever you want in the interview, if you think it is important.		
9. Always have more than one person interview a candidate.		

Sample Skills (not a complete list)

Ability to learn	Listening
Agility	Making tough decisions
Analysis	Managing multiple tasks
Assertiveness	Marketing
Building rapport	Meeting management
Communication (written/oral)	Meets deadlines
Computer…. (be specific)	Money management
Conflict resolution	Motivating others
Creativity	Negotiation
Data gathering	Persistence
Decisiveness	Phone skills
Delegating	Physical strength/endurance
Detail oriented	Planning and organizing
Developing others	Presentation skills
Energy	Prioritizing
Facilitation skills	Problem solving
Flexible thinking	Researching
Following instructions	Sales skills
Following procedures	Self motivation
Following safety rules	Sensitivity
Forward thinking	Teamwork
Giving instructions	Technical…. (be specific)
Initiative	Tenacity
Innovation	Troubleshooting
Interpreting blueprints, maps	Word processing (typing)
Leadership	Work under stress

Skill / Questions Interview Template

Job Title:

Required Skills:

Skill:

Question 1:

Question 2:

Question 3:

Skill:

Question 1:

Question 2:

Question 3:

Skill:

Question 1:

Question 2:

Question 3:

Resources

Americans with Disabilities Act (ADA)

Information and technical assistance on the Americans with Disabilities Act from the U.S. Department of Justice.

800-514-0301

TTY: 800-514-0383

www.ada.gov

American Society for Training and Development (ASTD)

ASTD is a professional association for people with training and development responsibilities in business, industry, education, government, public service, and other arenas of human resource development.

1640 King Street / Box 1443

Alexandria, VA 22313

800.628.2763

703.683.8100

www.ASTD.org

Bureau of National Affairs (BNA)

The BNA is a Washington, DC-based publisher of news and information on legislation, regulations, and court decisions for professionals in business and government.

1231–25th Street NW

Washington, DC 20037

800.372.1033

www.bna.com

California Department of Fair Employment and Housing (DFEH)

The mission of the Department of Fair Employment and Housing is to protect the people of California from unlawful discrimination in employment, housing, and public accommodations, and from the perpetration of acts of hate violence.

2000 O Street, Suite 120

Sacramento, CA 95814

800.952.5210

www.dfehmp.ca.gov

Job Accommodation Network

A resource for identifying possible accommodations in the workplace. A free consulting service of the Office of Disability Employment Policy, U.S. Dept. of Labor, designed to increase the employability of people with disabilities by 1) providing individualized worksite accommodation solutions, 2) providing technical assistance regarding the ADA and other disability related legislation, and 3) educating callers about self-employment options.

800.526.7234

TTY: 877.781.9403

www.jan.wvu.edu/

National Human Resources Association (NHRA)

The National Human Resources Association is focused on advancing the development of HR professionals.

P.O. Box 7326

Nashua, NH 03060–7326

Toll-Free: 866.523.4417

Fax: 603.891.5760

info@humanresources.org

www.humanresources.org

NOLO

The nation's oldest and most respected provider of legal information for consumers and small businesses.

www.NOLO.com (under Human Resources)

Society for Human Resource Management (SHRM)

SHRM provides a wide range of educational seminars and other activities that allow members to develop their expertise in the various functional areas that constitute human resource management.

1800 Duke Street

Alexandria, VA 23314

703.548.3440

www.shrm.org

Uniform Guidelines

These guidelines incorporate a single set of principles which are designed to assist employers, labor organizations, employment agencies, and licensing and certification boards to comply with requirements of Federal law prohibiting employment practices which discriminate on grounds of race, color, religion, sex, and national origin. They are designed to provide a framework for determining the proper use of tests and other selection procedures.

www.UniformGuidelines.com

U.S. Department of Labor (DOL)

The Department of Labor fosters and promotes the welfare of the job seekers and wage earners of the United States by improving their working conditions. In carrying out this mission, the Department administers a variety of Federal labor laws including those that guarantee workers' rights to safe and healthful working conditions, freedom from employment discrimination, and much more.

Frances Perkins Building

200 Constitution Avenue, NW

Washington, DC 20210

866.4.USA.DOL

TTY: 877.889.5627

www.dol.gov

U.S. Equal Employment Opportunity Commission (EEOC)

The Equal Employment Opportunity Commission, or EEOC, is a federal agency tasked with ending employment discrimination in the United States.

1801 L Street NW

Washington, DC 20507

800.669.4000

202.663.4900

www.eeoc.gov

About Janis Whitaker . . .

Janis Whitaker is the proud owner of J P Whitaker & Associates, a results-oriented management training and consulting enterprise since 1991. Janis has been a workplace learning and development professional since 1977. She was a Corporate Trainer/Supervisor in a medical manufacturing environment for seven years. As a trainer and consultant, she has experience working in a variety of workplace environments.

Currently, J P Whitaker & Associates present the following subject areas: Interviewing, Leadership, Communication Styles, Business Presentation Skills, Interpersonal Communication, Meeting Management, and Human Resource Skills.

Her subtle humor, personable style, and seasoned professionalism set her apart as a very sought after trainer.

In addition to corporate training, Janis was an adjunct faculty member at the University of Phoenix and has taught at University of California at San Diego and San Diego State University. She has been a guest presenter at many professional organizations. The American Society for Training and Development/San Diego has distinguished Janis Whitaker as "The Trainer's Trainer."

Janis has been an active member in Toastmasters International and has earned the Competent Toastmaster Level. Janis is also active in the American Society for Training and Development, San Diego Society for Human Resource Management, North County Personnel Association, and other professional organizations in her community.

Please see www.jpwhitaker.com for more information about J P Whitaker & Associates and the results-oriented workshops they offer.

J P Whitaker & Associates

Made in the USA
San Bernardino, CA
23 January 2017